Betsy Olmsted

HAND PRINTING STUDIO

A Visual Guide to Printing on Almost Anything

WITHDRAWN

15 Projects to Color Your Life

stashBOOKS.

an imprint of C&T Publishing

Text copyright © 2016 by Betsy Olmsted

Photography and artwork copyright © 2016 by C&T Publishing, Inc.

PUBLISHER: Amy Marson

CREATIVE DIRECTOR: Gailen Runge

EDITOR: Lynn Koolish

TECHNICAL EDITORS: Julie Waldman and Gailen Runge

COVER/BOOK DESIGN: Page + Pixel

PRODUCTION COORDINATOR: Tim Manibusan

PRODUCTION EDITORS: Alice Mace Nakanishi and Jessie Brotman

ILLUSTRATOR: Aliza Shalit

PHOTOGRAPHY by Sara Code Kroll, unless otherwise noted

INSTRUCTIONAL PHOTO STYLING by Betsy Olmsted and Sara Code Kroll

Published by Stash Books, an imprint of C&T Publishing, Inc., P.O. Box 1456, Lafayette, CA 94549

Library of Congress Cataloging-in-Publication Data

Names: Olmsted, Betsy, 1980-

Title: Hand-printing studio : 15 projects to color your life--a visual guide to printing on almost anything / Betsy Olmsted.

Description: Lafayette, California : C&T Publishing, Inc., [2016]

Identifiers: LCCN 2015038461 | ISBN 9781617451478 (soft cover)

Subjects: LCSH: Relief printing. | Screen process printing. | Decoration and ornament. | Handicraft.

Classification: LCC TT866.53 .O46 2016 | DDC 747--dc23

LC record available at http://lccn.loc.gov/2015038461

Printed in China

10 9 8 7 6 5 4 3 2 1

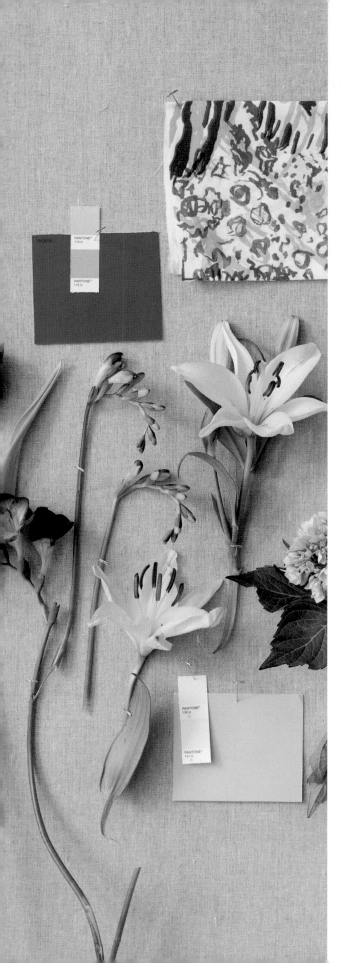

ACKNOWLEDGMENTS

I could not have accomplished this book without the help and support of others. Many special thanks to ...

- My children, Emmett and Wells, for sharing me with the studio and for their artistic contributions and modeling cooperation

- My husband, Peter, for his love and support

- Nicole Michels, of Bird & Banner, my unofficial consultant

- Ed and Nance, my parents, for providing us with a full-service studio space, including lunch delivery and home-grown celery, in their beautiful home

- Joanna Davis, for making the amazing Rodent Magnet as a birthday gift and for listening to all my creature woes

- Sara Code Kroll, CODE, my lovely friend and perfectly talented photographer who brought the book to life. We make a great team, and I hope to do it again!

- Baby Maeva—not for cooperating during your photo shoot but for allowing us to bother you! Your company was loved during all the photo shoots, both inside and outside of Mommy.

- Hitoshi Ujiie, of Philadelphia University, for telling me "to make the crap" and for your printing expertise

- Roxane Cerda, for visiting my booth at the Country Living Fair and giving me the encouragement and opportunity to work with C&T Publishing

- Lynn Koolish and Kristy Zacharias, for their confidence in me and their editorial direction in designing this book

- Katharine Karnaky, who would be my full-time life manager if she had not moved to California

- Rogan Motter—not necessarily for helping with the book but for helping with mostly everything else so that I could write it

- Michelle Johnsen, Erin Dorney, and Deb Grothe, for your assistance during photo shoots

DEDICATION

~ For Nance, my #1 fan ~

CONTENTS

HAND-PRINTING STUDIO

INTRODUCTION

Having always wanted to write a book, but having too many ideas as to what it would be, I am so happy to say, "Here it is!" My favorite part of working on this book was the photography shoots. I remember saying countless times to Sara, my friend and photographer, that I could not believe we managed to capture such neat and clean process images, while being surrounded by so much studio chaos! Do not be intimidated by the photos; you will make a mess while printing. Some of the things you do not see are all the masking tape stuck to the back of the tablecloth and the piles of unwashed spatulas, spoons, and palettes. I hope that this book brings hand printing into your life and that you will enjoy experimenting, creating, and making a mess. Happy printing!

> **NOTE**
> Important! The designs included in this book are only for your personal use and for donation to non-profit organizations. They may not be used for personal profit.

8

CREATING DESIGNS

9

One of the most common questions I am asked is, "How do you come up with your ideas?" For me the difficulty is not finding ideas but trying to narrow them! Too many ideas come from simply observing the everyday world. If a squirrel has been digging up my garden, then I paint his portrait. Weeds take over, so I pluck and sketch them. Listening to the imaginations of my children and absorbing their insatiable curiosity helps make the everyday enriching. I am drawn to an array of colors and textures that change through the seasons—so much of my work is inspired by nature. I also adore gathering objects and specimens, as you will see in these photographs. Allow the ins and outs of your daily life to inspire your designs and tell the story of you. Although this book includes patterns of my work for you to use, I hope you will experiment in coming up with your own!

DESIGNING FOR PRINTING

While you are drawing your design, it is a good idea to envision how it will look printed. Will it be one color or two or three? How will it be printed? On what will it be printed? Will it be a repeating pattern? Knowing the answers to these questions from the beginning may help you create the design. Sometimes I come up with the design first and then decide how it should be printed. After I created the rooster for This Little Rooster Went to Market (page 66), I knew that he was for kitchen items. The kaftan for Fluttering Kaftan (page 72) was designed first, and then I decided on the appropriate print for the finished piece.

TYPES OF DESIGNS

Understanding types of designs will help you figure out where to start and can also help you organize ideas and plan collections. Creating at least one design from each of the traditional genres is a starting method for developing prints that can be mixed and matched. The photos that follow are of designs that I have created over the years.

TIP

If you really want to be inspired, the book *Textile Designs: Two Hundred Years of European and American Patterns Organized by Motif, Style, Color, Layout, and Period*, by Susan Meller and Joost Elffers, is the quintessential textile reference bible and is great for coming up with ideas.

GEOMETRIC

Characterized by shapes you probably remember from geometry class, these designs do not need to be mathematically correct, symmetrical, or even drawn straight. Hand drawn or crooked can be charming and the simplest type of design to make.

CONVERSATIONAL

Conversational designs consist of recognizable motifs such as people, animals, seashells, fruits, and objects. Novelties and toiles fall into this category. A lot of my designs are conversational, since I love to draw and paint animals.

ABSTRACT

Although abstract designs depict unrecognizable forms, they can be representations of a particular subject. Simple shapes, marks, textures, and washes can be abstract.

FLORAL

As their name suggests, floral designs are renderings of flowers and plants. They can be simple, complex, or even geometric.

TECHNIQUES

Some of the best advice I have received about creating designs was from my professor and friend Hitoshi Ujiie at Philadelphia University: "Just make the crap!" So that is what I do—typically piles and piles of it. The purpose of putting ideas on paper is not to create precious masterpieces but to get an idea of the look you are after and to continue to work with it until you are happy. My favorite medium for designing is watercolor, but markers, pens, and pencils work just as well. It is best for the finished designs to be in black and white; if your design is multicolor, trace over it on tracing paper using a marker. If the final design ends up on tracing paper, that is okay—just make a photocopy. The following techniques are tricks for creating designs that can be printed.

FREE SKETCHING

This is the loosest, most organic technique. Simply observe what you would like to draw and sketch it on paper. It's easy to pick up fruits, vegetables, and flowers from the store or farmers' market. Surface designers love to stylize their subjects, so it does not have to look realistic to be a successful design.

TRACING A PHOTOGRAPH

Having photos from travels and life's inspirations on hand is a great jumping off point for creating designs. For a subject that is tricky to draw, try tracing a picture. I find that this is a great way to do animals. (In the photo, I'm using pictures from our county fair.) Make sure that your picture is large enough for you to trace detailed areas. Trace the outlines with a fine-tip marker and fill in solid areas with a broad-tip. I usually have to do this many times before landing on the final design.

TRACING FOUND OBJECTS

Tracing found objects is best for simple geometrics and simple silhouettes. Between my son's nature collection and our overflowing junk drawers and crammed basement, I have no shortage of interesting objects. Flat objects with interesting shapes can be traced to create designs including leaves, flowers, feathers, jewelry, coins, and tools. The top openings and bases of containers and glasses also work well.

USING YOUR CHILD'S ARTWORK

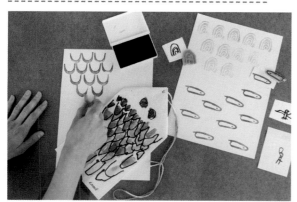

A collection of children's artwork requires an overwhelming amount of storage space. Choosing your favorites from your child's collection of artwork and preserving them through print will help the originals seem less precious (so you don't have to keep so many). Or, have your child create the artwork specifically for the print. I gave my son 3″ paper squares and had him draw simple designs with a marker. Seeing his drawings turned into stamps caused him much excitement!

COLOR

My passion for using bright, bold colors means that most of my designs are multicolor because I end up adding nearly every color to my palette. However, most of the designs in this book call for only one or two colors. Although the projects call for specific colors, please experiment in mixing your own. Neutrals and earthy tones can easily be substituted for the saturated hues I have selected.

SELECTING COLORS

There are so many choices that selecting a color can feel overwhelming. Refer to an image or a theme to narrow the spectrum to create a color story, which could be inspired by ideas such as the hues of your garden, shoe collection, or children's toys. If you are making a caftan, select colors you would wear. If you are printing a pillow, use colors that go with your decor. Try the unexpected. Chickens can be orange, and squirrels look nice in green. Simply picking colors that you like without thinking too much works well too.

MIXING COLORS

Even my five-year-old can mix colors. The most important thing to understand is basic primary and secondary color mixing. To avoid having to mix custom colors, you can find premixed inks in an array of colors. To mix colors you must have primaries—red, blue, and yellow—or process colors—cyan, yellow, and magenta—on hand. These process colors can be mixed in the same way as primaries but will yield slightly different hues. I also like to use cyan and magenta unmixed and straight out of the tube. Combinations of these colors produce shades of green, orange, and purple, the secondary colors. All colors can be lightened by adding clear base extender or white. I generally stay away from using white as an extender because it tends to dull the colors, though it can be added for a more opaque look.

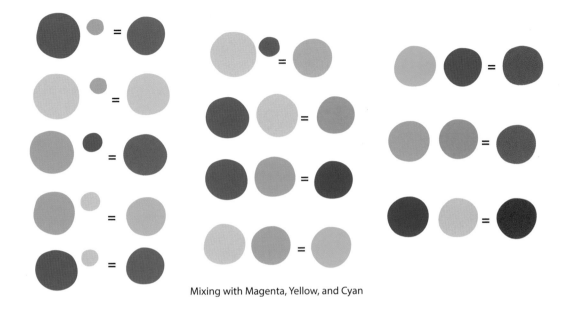

Mixing with Magenta, Yellow, and Cyan

These charts are reference guides to mixing approximate colors. Depending on the ink, dye, or brand, the colors will vary. Some manufacturers offer a color-mixing guide specific to their product.

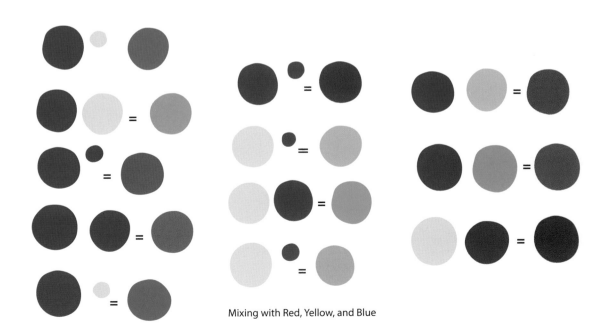

Mixing with Red, Yellow, and Blue

DESIGN REPEATS

Repeating—or printing a design over and over again on the same surface—can be as simple or complex as you would like. Although some of the projects in this book call for repeats, the nature of hand printing is organic, irregular, and sometimes primitive, so "mistakes" can sometimes be charming.

There are, however, specific layouts for printing designs as a pattern. These methods are used throughout this book and can help you arrange the layout of your own designs. After you have decided on a drawing, try photocopying it at least four times; then cut out the images and move them around in different layouts so you can plan your printing placement.

STRAIGHT MATCH

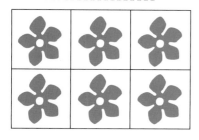

HALF DROP

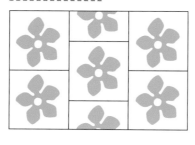

RANDOM

20

SURFACES, INKS, DYES, MATERIALS, AND TOOLS

Before printing, you must select the appropriate surface and colorant combination. Inks and colors may be specific to a certain type of printing method and surface, so planning ahead is necessary.

TYPES OF FIBERS

It is helpful to understand what fabrics are made of, so that you can select the correct dye or ink for your project. Fabrics are made of fibers, which may originate from a natural source, such as plants and animals, or they may be manufactured/synthetic. Sometimes the fibers can be blended. Make sure to read the content labels of any fabric you are planning to purchase for these projects. The casual and organic nature of cotton and linen, as well as the variety of textures and weights available, make these fabrics my favorite choices for printing projects.

PLANT FIBERS

Otherwise known as cellulose, these fibers originate from plants and include cotton, linen, hemp, flax, rayon, modal, jute, bamboo, and ramie. Organic versions of these fabrics are also available, meaning they were grown without the use of pesticides.

ANIMAL FIBERS

Known as protein fibers, these come from animals and include wool, hair, and silk. Organic wool and silk are available, which means the animals and silkworms were raised on organic foods.

SYNTHETIC FIBERS

Synthetic fibers are manufactured mostly from petroleum products. They include polyester, acetate, nylon, olefin, and polypropylene.

FABRICS

The appearance of your print will change from fabric to fabric. Textures and weight vary between different fibers and according to how the fabric was made.

french terry

polyester sheer

natural linen

cotton gauze

muslin- white

muslin- natural

cotton canvas

cotton slub

indoor/outdoor poly

cotton linen blend

polyester felt

quilting cotton

WOVENS

Plain-weave fabrics, such as canvas and muslin, work well for printing because of their smooth texture. Woven fabrics do not have much stretch and tend to soften with wear. Wovens are great for pillows, aprons, tea towels, structured clothing, quilts, and scarves.

KNITS

Knits have much more stretch than wovens and come in a variety of styles and weights. Interlock, jersey, and French terrycloth are good for printing because of their smooth surface. Softness makes knits perfect for baby items such as blankets, sheets, and clothing. Presewn items, such as T-shirts and sweatshirts, are great for printing. Many knits are 100% cotton, but lots are a cotton/polyester blend. Although slightly difficult to find, knit linen has a naturally irregular texture that is great for apparel.

NONWOVENS

Nonwoven fabrics, such as felt, which is usually made from wool or a synthetic, are neither woven nor knit.

OTHER PRINTABLE MATERIALS

GLASS

Commercially, glass can be printed with industrial inks formulated for glass and other nonporous surfaces. For home crafters, glass paint works well, and its transparency makes it appear as though the color is melted on glass. Use small stamps, as the glass surface can be slippery.

METAL

As with glass, metal is printed commercially with industrial inks. For printing at home, oil-based block-printing ink is the way to go, as it finishes with a smooth, transparent coverage.

WOOD

Variations in wood grain, species, and color really help make printed pieces of wood one of a kind. Wood with a smooth surface works the best for both block and screen printing. Panels, boards, boxes, and veneer cards or sheets are all suitable items for printing.

PAPER

Finding your paper of choice requires some experimenting. High-quality cardstock works well, as do many types of printmaking paper. Smooth surfaces are needed for even ink coverage. Trying colored stocks can be fun.

SKIN

Printing on skin is a temporary alternative to tattoos. All you need is a willing subject; you may end up with more than you hoped for!

INKS AND DYES

PIGMENTS / WATER-BASED INKS

The terms *water-based inks* and *pigments* are interchangeable and refer to a type of colorant that bonds to the surface after being set with heat. Water-based inks can be used on all fabric types and work best with screen printing, although they can also be block printed. These inks are available in premixed containers from Speedball or Versatex or as base extender and color concentrates from PRO Chemical & Dye (see Resources, page 111). Concentrates are very strong, and sometimes only a few drops are needed in the extender. These inks need to be heat set with an iron or commercial dryer according to the manufacturer's directions.

BLOCK-PRINTING INKS FOR FABRIC

Speedball makes a wonderful block-printing ink for fabric, available in a variety of premixed colors. It is oil based but cleans up with soap and water. It does dry quickly, so wait to mix them until you're ready to print. I always add base extender to soften the colors. These inks require one week of air curing.

OIL-BASED BLOCK-PRINTING INKS

Also made by Speedball, these inks work on surfaces such as metal, wood, and paper. Mineral spirits or turpentine are required for cleanup. Allow one week for curing.

ACRYLIC SCREEN-PRINTING INKS

These superconcentrated, premixed colors work on paper and wood and are available from companies such as Speedball. The extender has a gluelike consistency, and you should expect to use plenty of it when mixing colors. Sometimes it takes this ink a few minutes of mixing to "warm it up," especially if the storage area is chilly.

INKS/DYES	PRINT TYPES	SURFACES	INFORMATION	CLEANUP	CURING	BRANDS
Acrylic screen-printing ink	Screen printing	Paper and wood	Find color in premixed tubs and add to base extender.	Soap and water	Air dry	Speedball
Discharge paste	Block and screen printing and hand painting	Dyed cotton, linen, or rayon	Removes the color from fabric; be sure to test a sample first.	Soap and water	Steam	Jacquard, Harbor Sales
Disperse dyes	Transfer printing	Polyester or nylon	Powdered dyes that mix with water to form watercolor paint. Wear a dust mask when handling dye powder.	Soap and water	Heat transfer	PRO Chemical & Dye's PRO Transperse Dye
Glass paint	Block printing	Glass	Purchase as a multicolor set in small plastic tubs.	Soap and water	Air dry	—
Oil-based block-printing Ink	Block printing	Wood, metal, or paper	Colors are available in tubes.	Mineral spirits or turpentine	Air dry	Speedball
Tattoo ink	Block printing	Skin	Pre-inked stamp pad	Soap and water	Air dry	Memories
Textile block-printing ink	Block printing	All fabrics, wood, and paper	Available in color tubes and transparent base extender. It tends to dry quickly, so a retarder can be added.	Soap and water	Air dry	Speedball
Water-based inks	Screen printing, hand painting, stamping, and block printing	All fabrics	Available as premixed colors or can be purchased as color concentrates with transparent base.	Soap and water	Heat set according to package instructions	PRO Chemical & Dye, Versatex

EXTENDER

Extender is available for water-based inks, acrylic screen-printing inks, and block-printing inks. Color concentrates or premixed colors can be added to clear extender to lighten the color and make it more transparent. Colors can also be added to white extender to make them more pastel. Mostly, I avoid using the white base because I like my colors to be vibrant and to look like dye—I think white tends to be dulling.

DISPERSE DYES

Disperse dyes are very colorfast, since they actually dissolve into the fibers of synthetic fabrics. In this book, these dyes will be used for transfer printing on nylon and polyester. Available as powders, they can be mixed with water to make watercolor paints. Wear a dust mask when mixing powdered dyes, as the smell can be a bit offensive. PRO Chemical & Dye offers a basic transfer printing kit, which is what I used for the projects in this book.

DISCHARGE PASTE

Discharge paste (made by Jacquard) or deColourant (by Harbor Sales) removes color and can be screen printed or block printed onto predyed cotton, linen, or rayon. After drying, it must be heat set or steamed to begin its bleaching effect. Test the fabric first, as some colors will not respond to the discharge as well as others do.

TEMPORARY TATTOO STAMPING INKS

This ink is available in pre-inked stamp pads in a variety of colors and can last for a few days. Allow about ten minutes to dry to prevent smudging.

PREPARING TO PRINT

PREPARING THE FABRIC

Always wash the fabric before printing to remove starches and sizings. This will help inks adhere more strongly.

WORK SURFACES

Practically any flat, smooth surface will work for printing. I recommend using a board, such as cork or Homasote wall boards from the hardware store, cut to the size of the tabletop. Place the board on a tabletop and cover it with a canvas drop cloth so that you can tack down the fabric being printed to prevent it from slipping.

PATTERNS

Patterns of my work are included in this book and can be used for personal use and for donations to nonprofit organizations only. They may not be used to make items for sale. Always use photocopies of your patterns to preserve the original for future use.

CRAFT KNIVES

A craft knife, such as an X-ACTO, is used throughout this book. If you are a beginner, do not expect to be a perfect cutter. Practice to get the hang of it. Hold the knife like a pencil and always make sure that your blade is sharp; you may need to change blades frequently. When cutting a thick material, don't try to cut all the way through in one cut; two or three cuts will probably be necessary.

CUTTING MATS

Cut on a self-healing cutting mat when using a craft knife. The mat will help prevent the blade from dulling too quickly, and its printed grid will make cutting straight lines easier.

PRACTICING, TESTING, AND SAMPLING

Always test print on a scrap surface before printing the final piece. You need to make sure the color is correct and that the texture is okay. Testing will also help you become comfortable with the technique. Expect mistakes and errors, which sometimes can be happy accidents. Print lots of items at a time and choose the best for use.

SEWING

The sewing instructions in this book are simple and include basic patterns. If you do not sew, that is okay! Take the printed pieces to someone who does, such as an alterations shop, and show them the instructions. Printing on presewn blanks can be a good option, but printing over already-sewn hems usually does not yield the best results.

BLOCK PRINTING

I love block printing because of the wide variety of surfaces that can be printed; the process is easy, and cleanup is a snap.

My first experience with block printing, which is essentially the same as stamping, was as a student visiting the village of Bagru, India, where fifth-generation carvers and printers work in the historic tradition. Blocks are carved from wood, and most printing is done with vegetable dyes. Projects in this book are in the spirit of traditional block printing but are simplified for use with readily available modern materials. I love block printing because of the wide variety of surfaces that can be printed; the process is easy, and cleanup is a snap. Blocks can be used over and over again and mixed and matched to create new designs. Printing does not need to be perfect. Variations in placement and ink coverage add to the charm. Blocks last and last and can be used for many different projects!

TOOLS AND MATERIALS

BLOCKS

The block-printing projects require cutting custom blocks made of a soft rubber material. They come with names such as Speedy-Carve Blocks (Speedball) or soft block in shades of pink, blue, and white. Using a soft material rather than traditional linoleum is best for the projects in this book. Not only is it easier to carve, but the ability to completely remove the design from the edges makes it easier to line up repeats and see exactly where the image is falling on the surface.

BRAYERS

A brayer is a rolling cylinder on a handle used for applying ink to a carved block. It is good to have a few sizes on hand.

CARVING TOOLS

Block-carving tools or lino-carving tools are used to cut a design into a block. A set typically includes about five blades and a handle. Fine blades are used for carving detailed areas, and wider blades are for clearing away large areas. Do not expect to carve perfectly the first time. Practice with all the blades, experimenting with curves and angles, before carving your final design.

BURNISHING TOOL

A burnishing tool, or bone folder, is long and flat and somewhat resembles a letter opener. It is used for transferring designs drawn in pencil and for smoothing surfaces.

TRANSFERRING THE DESIGN

Materials

- Rubber carving block
- Soft pencil, such as 5B
- Burnishing tool
- Copy paper

Instructions

1 Photocopy the Crochet design pattern (page 101) or design your own.

2 Trace the outline of the design on the photocopy with a soft pencil.

3 Transfer the design to the block by placing the paper facedown on the block and rubbing with a burnishing tool until the pencil lines appear on the block.

4 Lift the paper.

CARVING THE BLOCK

Materials

- Rubber carving block with transferred design
- Carving tools
- Craft knife, such as an X-ACTO
- Cutting mat

Instructions

1 Using one of the V-shaped carving tools, carve around the design's silhouette.

2 Remove the area around the design by carving away from the design and away from yourself.

3 Use a fine V-shaped tool to carve away detailed areas.

4 Remove the area around the edges with a craft knife or precision scissors.

TIPS

BLOCK CARVING

- Always test and experiment when trying a new process! Practice with carving tools on a scrap before carving the final block. Remember, positive areas will be inked and negative areas will be cut or carved away.

- Always carve *away* from the design. That way, if the tool slips, the design will not be damaged.

- For carving curves and corners, try turning the block instead of turning your wrist.

- Carve slowly and gently.

PRINTING WITH THE BLOCK

Materials

- Carved block
- Ink and base extender (see Inks and Dyes, page 26)
- Soft rubber brayer
- Inking plate or palette

INK THE PALETTE

Squeeze the desired colors and base extender onto a palette. The palette should be a smooth, flat, washable surface, such as a piece of Plexiglas.

INK THE BRAYER

Roll the brayer through the ink and repeat in the same direction until the brayer is evenly covered and colors are thoroughly mixed.

INK THE STAMP

Roll the brayer over the stamp design until it is evenly coated.

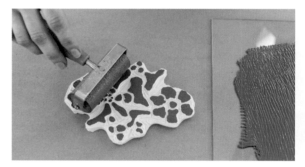

PRINT

1 Turn the stamp over onto the printing surface. Apply even pressure with the palms of your hand on all areas of the stamp.

2 Hold the stamp firmly in place for at least 10 seconds and do not allow the stamp to shift; otherwise, the print will smear.

CROCHET PRINTED TABLE RUNNER

Laces and doilies abound at local flea and antique markets. They remind me of the Victorian bedroom at my grandmother's house, which was like stepping into a primitive time past. This runner pays homage to the old but is updated for modern use. To make matching items, print on 20˝ × 20˝ squares for napkins or a throw pillow!

Materials

- Natural color linen: ½ yard × 60″ wide
- Rubber block
- Soft pencil, such as 5B
- Carving tools
- Burnishing tool
- Permanent marker with fine tip
- Craft knife, such as an X-ACTO
- Fabric block-printing ink in magenta and extender (or a color of your choice)
- Inking plate or palette
- Sewing machine and thread

Instructions

Refer to Block Printing (page 31).

1 Transfer the Crochet design pattern (page 101) to the block.

2 Cut out the designs with carving tools and craft knife.

3 Mark the back of the stamp in the top, bottom, and left side so you can see where the repeat will line up.

4 Place the fabric across the printing table.

5 Ink the palette using about a teaspoon of magenta textile block-printing ink and a tablespoon of extender.

6 Ink the brayer.

7 Ink the stamp.

8 Print the linen by starting in the upper left side and moving down the fabric vertically.

9 Line up the repeat according to the marks on the back of the stamp and continue to print.

10 Clean the brayers and stamps with soap and water and allow the ink to cure for 1 week.

11 Fold under the edges ¼″ twice and stitch a hem.

TOMATO THIEF ACCENT PILLOW

Word seemed to be out among all neighborhood rodents to wreak havoc in my life, as my four years of attempting to grow tomatoes always ended in disaster. I vowed to keep trying, but then the squirrel came. During the final escapade, one tomato was ripening on the vine. My son and I checked on it every day, just waiting for it to turn red. One morning it was gone! A few hours later I looked into the hemlock trees nearby, and there was my tomato! A squirrel had stolen it and placed it in plain view, seeming to laugh at us.

Materials

- Cotton canvas
- Rubber carving block
- Soft pencil, such as 5B
- Carving tools
- Craft knife, such as an X-ACTO, or precision scissors
- Fabric scissors
- Fabric block-printing inks in turquoise, yellow, magenta, and extender (or colors of your choice)
- Soft rubber brayer
- Inking plate or palette
- Polyfill stuffing
- Sewing machine and thread

Instructions

Refer to Block Printing (page 31).

1 Transfer the Sneaky Squirrel pattern and Tomato pattern (page 102) to the block. The Tomato pattern should be transferred separately to either a corner of the squirrel block or a scrap of block material.

2 Carve the blocks with carving tools and precision scissors or a craft knife.

3 Place the fabric folded in half on the work surface and place the squirrel block on top. Loosely trace the silhouette of the block onto the fabric, leaving about 2˝ between the block and the marker line. This will be the shape of the pillow.

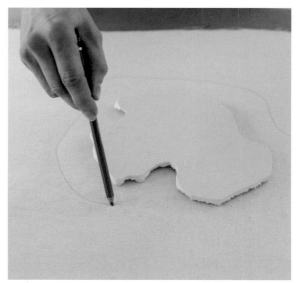

4 Cut the shape from the fabric through both layers, so you end up with 2 pieces.

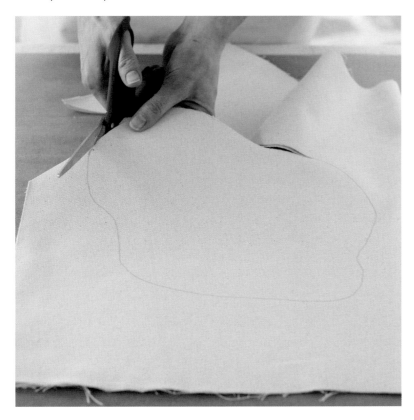

5 Place a piece from Step 4 on the working surface.

6 Ink the palette with about 1 teaspoon yellow, ¼ teaspoon blue, a tiny spot of magenta, and 1 teaspoon extender on the palette.

7 Ink the brayer and mix the inks.

8 Ink the stamp.

9 Print the squirrel in the center of the fabric.

10 Print the tomato by following Steps 6–9 but replacing the colors with ½ teaspoon magenta, ⅛ teaspoon yellow, and ½ teaspoon extender.

11 Clean the brayers and stamps with soap and water and allow the print to cure for 1 week.

12 Sew the pieces together and stuff the pillow. Once the print has cured, pin the print and the second fabric piece, right sides together.

13 Sew around the outside with a ¼″ seam allowance, leaving a 3″ opening at the bottom for turning.

14 Clip the curves and points of the seam allowance if you wish.

15 Turn the pillow right side out and stuff with polyfill. Hand stitch the opening closed.

TOMATO THIEF ACCENT PILLOW

TRIANGLED COFFEE TABLE

Finding the perfect coffee table took me hours of online research that ended with nothing to show. So I decided to make my own that would not only suit the style and dimensions of our room but would also hold up to our family's lifestyle. Plus, a custom coffee table costs less than a purchased one. Neutral colors and simple geometrics paired with handmade hairpin legs will work in many spaces, and if you tire of the top, just print another!

Materials

- Birch or maple plywood: ¾″ thick, 24″ × 48″

- 14″ hairpin legs, spray-painted gold: 4 (see Resources, page 111)

- Oil-based block-printing ink in white (or a color of your choice)

- Soft pencil, such as 5B

- Rubber carving block

- Craft knife, such as an X-ACTO

- 12″ metal ruler

- Inking plate or palette

- Screws and screwdriver

- Very fine sandpaper (#220 or higher)

- Turpentine or turpentine substitute (I prefer Turpenoid brand.)

- Wax or oil wood finish

Instructions

Refer to Block Printing (page 31).

1 Transfer the Triangle Coffee Table pattern (page 103) to the block.

2 Cut out the triangle design with a craft knife.

3 Place the plywood on your printing table so it faces you horizontally.

4 Squeeze about 1 tablespoon of white ink onto your palette.

5 Ink the brayer.

6 Ink the stamp and print the plywood, beginning in the top left corner, so that the edge of the triangle reaches the edge of the surface.

7 Continue inking the stamp and printing in a row, so that the bottom corners are slightly touching. Print the second row by staggering the triangles. Print a total of 3 rows.

8 Print another 3 rows across the bottom so that it mirrors the top 3 rows.

9 Clean the brayer and stamp with turpentine.

10 Allow the ink to cure for 1 week.

11 Lightly sand the wood with very fine sandpaper until smooth (*optional*).

12 Assemble the table: Turn the printed wood upside down and screw the hairpin legs into the four corners, with an inset of about 2″.

13 Seal the surface and edges with wood oil or wax with a dry cloth according to the manufacturer's directions. Cure according to the manufacturer's instructions.

TRIANGLED COFFEE TABLE

FOLLOW THE SNAIL GALVANIZED BUCKET PLANTER

48

As a mother of two boys, I have spent countless hours hunting bugs and critters. Worms, fireflies, snails, caterpillars, inchworms, and salamanders are some of Emmett's and Wells' prized captures, and the first place to look for them is under our herb pots! It seems natural that these creatures should adorn the sides of a bucket planter as a reminder of what may live underneath.

Materials

- Galvanized metal bucket with smooth sides
- Rubber carving block (The thinner pink kind will print better on a curved surface.)
- Oil-based block-printing ink in turquoise and yellow (or colors of your choice)
- Soft rubber brayer
- Craft knife, such as an X-ACTO, or precision scissors
- Soft pencil, such as 5B
- Burnishing tool
- Carving tools
- Inking plate or palette
- Mineral spirits
- Potting soil
- Plants

Instructions

Refer to Block Printing (page 31).

1 Transfer the Snail pattern (page 103) to the block.

2 Carve the block with carving tools and precision scissors or craft knife.

3 Ink the palette with 1 teaspoon turquoise oil-based block-printing ink.

4 Ink the brayer. **5** Ink the stamp.

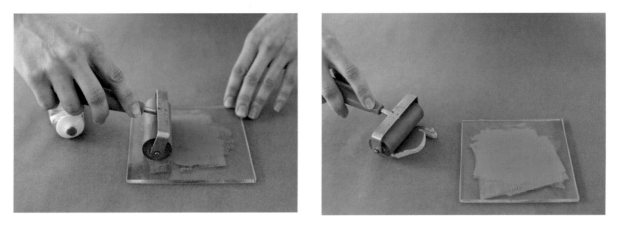

6 To print the planter, place the bucket on its side on a table or in your lap. Starting at the bottom, print the first row, spacing the snails about ¾″ apart.

7 Re-ink your stamp by adding yellow to the palette.

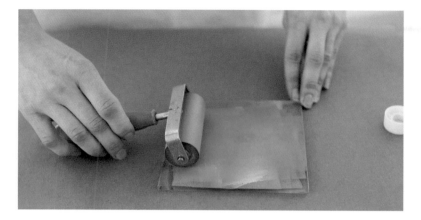

8 Print the second row so that the snails stagger into a half-drop position (see Design Repeats, page 19), about ½˝ above the first row.

9 Repeat Steps 7 and 8 for Row 3.

10 Allow the ink to cure for 1 week.

11 Use a screwdriver to drill or stab a few ½˝–1˝ holes in the bottom of the bucket to allow for drainage.

12 Fill the bucket with planting soil; add the plants.

CHEVRON ANTIQUE GLASS VASES

Vintage shopping is one of my favorite activities, and finding the perfect antique glass vessels gives this project individual character. I look for bottles that have an iridescent patina, similar to that of a bubble, and that can hold at least one stem. Allow the patina colors to guide your choices in paint color. Tiny stamps work best, since glass tends to be a slippery surface.

Materials

- 1–5 antique, clear glass vessels, bottles, or vases
- Rubber carving block
- Glass paint
- Small paintbrush
- Craft knife, such as an X-ACTO

Instructions

Refer to Block Printing (page 31).

1 Transfer the Tiny Chevron pattern (page 103) to the block.

2 Cut out the stamp with the craft knife.

4 Print the bottle. Depending on the bottle's size, you may be able to print multiple chevron shapes in vertical and horizontal directions.

5 Wash the stamp.

6 Allow the paint to dry.

7 Touch up with a brush and paint if desired.

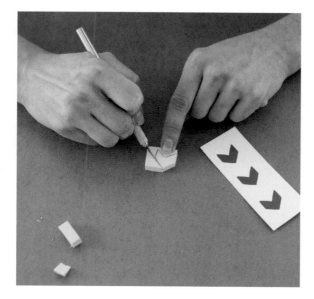

3 Paint the stamp with glass paint.

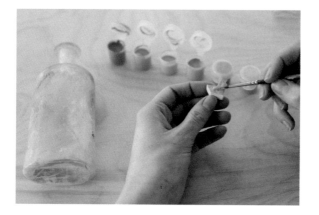

REPTILE
BIRD CHILDREN

My children love pretending to be animals. Birds, particularly raptors, and reptiles are some of their favorites. Emmett's imaginary friend is a blue-tailed hawk, and a chipmunk-eagle crashed into our window last week. So, when I discovered temporary tattoo stamp pads, I knew the boys would be excited to transform their little bodies into creatures! On the day that I printed the boys, a few minutes before we began, our neighbors magically caught a cute little garter snake and let us take it home. Emmett made sure that I followed the natural color palette of its scales while printing. The snake was very happy to be released in our garden that evening.

Materials

- A child or 2—or if children are not available, 1 willing adult

- Rubber carving block

- Temporary tattoo stamp ink in blue, green, and henna (or colors of your choice)

- Craft knife, such as an X-ACTO, or precision scissors

- Carving tools

- Soft pencil, such as 5B

Instructions

Refer to Block Printing (page 31).

1 Transfer the Scale/Feather pattern (page 103) to the block.

2 Carve the stamp with carving tools and the craft knife or precision scissors.

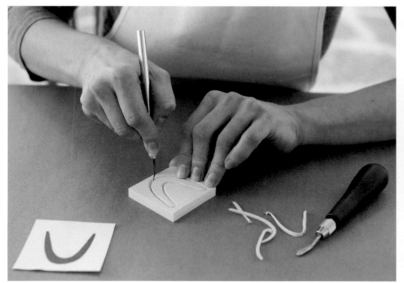

3 Ink the stamp by pressing it into a stamp pad.

4 Print the scale/feather stamp on the arms. Hold one arm at a time and begin printing with your choice of ink just below the shoulder. Print one scale on the top row, followed by alternating a row of 2 scales and a row of 3 scales. Do not print the underside of the arm. Randomly change stamp pad colors as desired.

5 Print the chest and back if desired. When printing the chest, start low enough so that the child's chin will not rub onto the printing.

6 The printed child should air dry for about 5 minutes to prevent smudging.

7 Close the stamp pad cases and rinse the stamp with soap and water.

REPTILE BIRD CHILDREN

SCREEN PRINTING

Most printed textiles you see have been screen printed. This process can be used for mass production of large volumes or printed by hand to create one-of-a-kind pieces with individual quirks and character.

TOOLS AND MATERIALS

Screen printing is the process of adhering a stencil to a fine mesh screen and pushing ink or dye through it and onto fabric, paper, or another surface. The projects in this book use screens that have been prestretched over wooden frames. Two different methods are used to apply the designs to the screen.

SILK SCREEN

A silk screen is polyester mesh fabric stretched over a wooden frame. The projects in this book call for prestretched wood or metal frames, which are available in craft stores and online. Stencils of designs are transferred to the screen using a number of methods prior to printing.

SQUEEGEE

A squeegee is used to pull ink across the screen in screen printing. Squeegees have rounded edges for fabrics and square edges for paper. When selecting the appropriate size squeegee, make sure it is at least the same width as the design being printed and not larger than the frame of the silk screen.

CREATING DESIGNS: PAPER STENCIL METHOD

This quick and easy method is best for simple cut shapes. The stencils cannot be reused, so it is best not to invest a lot of time in cutting the designs. Print a lot since you will throw away the stencil right away.

Materials

- Silk screen
- Copy paper
- Craft knife, such as an X-ACTO, or precision scissors
- Masking tape

Instructions

1 Photocopy your design onto copy paper.

2 Cut out the design with a craft knife or precision scissors.

3 Center the stencil on the outside of the screen and tape the edges to the screen frame.

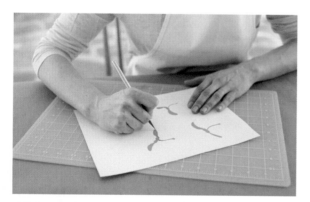

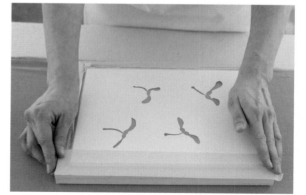

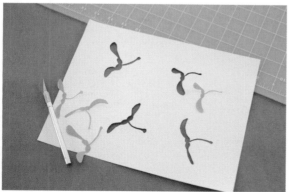

CREATING DESIGNS: SCREEN FILLER METHOD

Although very simple, this method allows for the most detail, and the screen can be washed and reused. Screen filler is painted directly onto the screen with a brush to create the image. The filler paints on smoothly around the design so that the ink will not pass through the painted areas after drying. I use Speedball Screen Filler. The screen filler can be removed if you make a mistake. If you want to use the screen for something else, you can use a product called Speedball Speed Clean.

Materials

- Silk screen
- Fabric squeegee
- Screen filler
- Paintbrushes
- Masking tape

TIP

Think of the silkscreen like the lid of a box; the inside is like the inside of the box, and the outside is like the outside of the box.

Instructions

1 Tape the copied design centered onto the *inside* of the screen.

2 Turn over the screen. Use screen filler to paint around the design on the white areas onto the outside of the screen; allow it to dry.

3 After the filler is dry, hold the screen up to the light and inspect it to make sure that all filled areas are fully covered. Touch up with a brush where necessary.

4 Once the design is fully dry, tape the screen around the design's border.

PRINTING WITH A SCREEN

Printing with a screen takes a little bit of practice, but you'll catch on quickly. If you are a beginner, try first with very simple artwork, so that you are not left frustrated with ruined stencils and designs. After you have the hang of it, gradually add more detail to your designs.

Materials

- Silk screen with artwork
- Fabric squeegee
- Screen-printing ink
- Printable surface, such as fabric, paper, or wood
- Plastic containers
- Plastic spatula
- Measuring cups and spoons

Instructions

1 Place the screen with artwork on top of the printing surface so that the top of the screen is to the left if you are right-handed or to right if you are left-handed.

2 Use a plastic spoon or plastic spatula to add ink vertically along top of the screen.

3 Hold the screen firmly in place with your left hand and hold the squeegee with your right hand. (If you're left-handed, you may want to reverse these instructions.)

4 Flood the screen: Place the squeegee above the ink and pull, at an angle, across the screen. Check to see if the screen is evenly coated, or flooded, with ink. You have just printed the first pass. Continue to hold the screen firmly in place.

5 Print the second pass by turning the squeegee and pushing the ink back in the other direction.

TIPS

• Make sure that the artwork is at least 1″ from the frame so that you have a place for the ink.

• Apply tape around the border of the design to prevent ink from getting through uncovered areas.

• Always apply designs to the *outside* of the screen frame.

• When printing with water-based inks, don't worry if you make a mistake. It will wash out if it is has not been heat set.

• Clean screens thoroughly! After the inks are dried, it is very difficult to remove them from the screen mesh; so wash up immediately following printing, preferably with a sprayer faucet.

THIS LITTLE ROOSTER WENT TO MARKET KITCHEN COLLECTION

Chickens and kitchens are a classic combination. This particular rooster was a prize winner at our local county fair. Printing in an unexpected color adds an unusual twist to traditional rooster designs. Try printing him on a variety of blanks or even in repeat.

HAND-PRINTING STUDIO

Materials

- Presewn flour sack tea towels, apron, and canvas tote (the "blanks")
- 9″ × 12″ silk screen
- Screen filler
- Fabric squeegee
- Water-based textile inks and clear base extender
- Plastic containers
- Masking tape

Instructions

Refer to Screen Printing (page 59).

1. Transfer the Rooster pattern (page 104) to the screen using the screen filler method (page 62).

2. Mix inks: Start with ¼ cup of base extender in a container. Add 2 drops of red and ½ teaspoon yellow and mix thoroughly.

3. Place the blanks on the printing surface.

4. Print blanks one at a time.

5. Wash the screen.

6. Heat set the ink after it is dry.

HEART OF WOOD VALENTINES

Since I was born on Valentine's Day, I have a special relationship with the holiday and love to receive special Valentine's Day / birthday cards and notes. Handmade valentines are the more personal way to show appreciation for loved ones and are super easy to make! These simple designs can be printed on wood or paper. Try using a variety of shapes and sizes, and experiment with placement and overlapping colors. The valentines will become keepsakes and can even be framed.

Materials

- 5″ × 7″ wood postcards or paper cards (I used curly maple.)
- 8″ × 10″ stretched silk screen
- Acrylic-based screen-printing inks and base extender
- Squeegee
- Plastic spoons
- Spatula
- Copy paper
- Scissors

Instructions

Refer to Screen Printing (page 59).

1 Make the paper stencils by folding a piece of copy paper in half and cutting out a heart shape with your choice of scissors. Cut a few with hearts of varying shapes and sizes, but all measuring roughly 3″ in length, or cut lots of little hearts.

2 Select the first stencil and tape it to the outside of the screen.

3 Mix the magenta color with 2 tablespoons extender and 1 teaspoon magenta directly onto the inside of the screen next to the design.

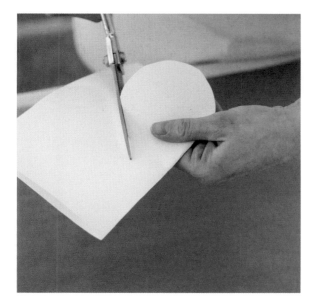

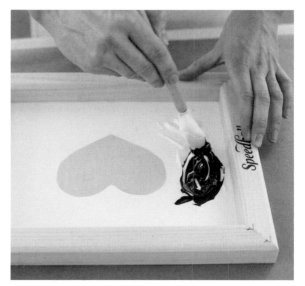

4 Print the magenta toward the bottom left side of a card or in many placement variations. Continue printing as many as you would like and allow to them dry. Wash and dry the screen and throw away the used stencil.

5 Select a heart stencil that is different in shape than the printed heart and tape it to the screen. Mix chartreuse directly on the screen using 2 tablespoons extender, 1 teaspoon yellow, and 2 dabs of blue.

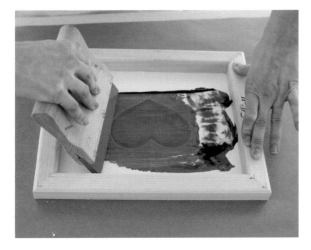

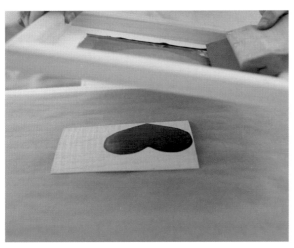

6 Print the chartreuse in varied positions, overlapping the magenta hearts.

7 Print a third color if you would like. For this project,
I used periwinkle: 2 tablespoons extender, ½ teaspoon blue,
and 3 dabs of magenta.

FLUTTERING KAFTAN

If the only article of clothing I was ever to wear were a kaftan, I would be very, very happy. I cannot get enough of these loose, flowing garments; so I devised a simple way to make my own to go easier on the wallet. This project calls for discharge printing, but feel free to use colored pigments and a variety of colored fabrics for a full range of options. Loose-weave cotton, such as gauze, works best for this particular sewing pattern. Maple pods cascade down the sides to enhance the mellow drape of the gauze.

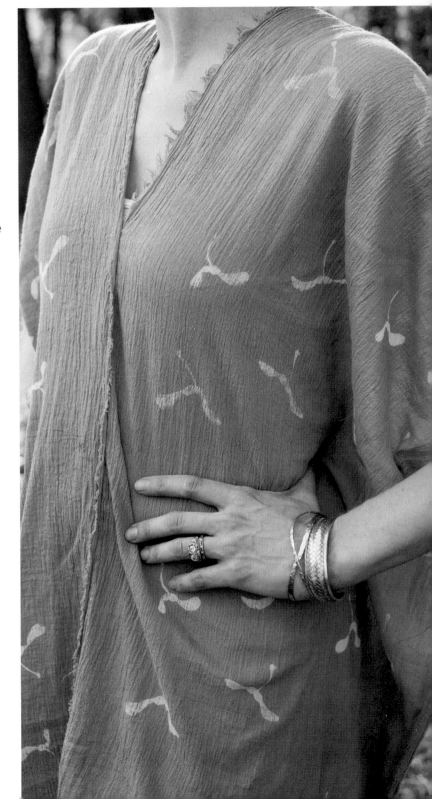

72

Materials

- Predyed cotton gauze fabric at least 42″ wide: 2 yards

- 8″ × 10″ silk screen

- Fabric squeegee

- Discharge paste such as Jacquard (see Discharge Paste, page 28)

- Masking tape

- Craft knife, such as an X-ACTO

- Cutting mat

- 8½″ × 11″ card stock

- Sewing machine and thread

TIPS

- Select a fabric with attractive selvages.

- Print the design about three times on a scrap piece before working on the final pieces.

- Adjust the size of your kaftan to make it wider or narrower or shorter.

- To make a kid's kaftan, reduce the size of the pieces to 10″ × 1½ yards. Alternatively, you can use textile paint rather than discharging.

- Try using two different colors of fabric for a color-blocked look.

- Print and steam discharge paste in a ventilated area; open windows work fine.

- Do not steam iron the paste until it is completely dry!

- Pretest discharge on the fabric you plan to use to make sure you like the result; it sometimes changes to unexpected colors.

- Discharge paste will only work on cotton, linen, or rayon.

Instructions

Refer to Screen Printing (page 59).

PRINT THE DESIGN

1 Make the stencil using the Kaftan Pods pattern (page 105).

2 Fold the fabric in half along its length. Place the fabric onto a large, flat surface.

3 Measure 18″ from each selvage toward the center; clip the fabric.

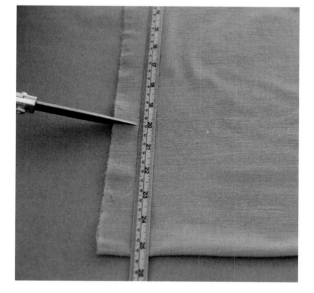

④ Gently tear at the marks, so that you have 2 pieces of equal size, each measuring 18″ × 2 yards, both with selvages. Use the leftover piece for testing prints.

⑤ Iron both pieces so they are smooth enough for printing.

⑥ Place a piece of fabric across the printing surface.

⑦ Pour the discharge paste directly onto the screen.

⑧ Print the design. Continue printing across the fabric randomly.

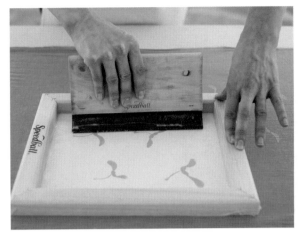

⑨ Repeat Steps 6–8 to print the second piece.

⑩ When both pieces are dry, iron on the cotton setting to activate the discharge paste.

ASSEMBLE THE KAFTAN

1 Place the pieces side by side so that one selvage overlaps the other by about ½˝.

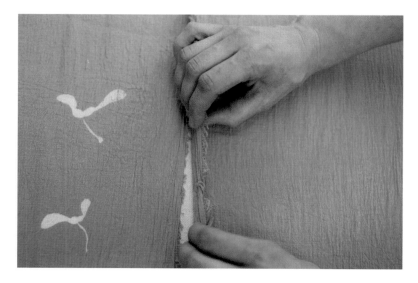

2 Mark the center.

3 Measure 9˝ in each direction from the center and pin. This is the neck opening.

4 Sew the pieces together by topstitching along the selvages using a straight stitch.

5 Turn the kaftan inside out and fold it in half crosswise. Measure 14˝ down from the fold for arm openings, and sew the remaining sides together.

6 Hem the bottom by turning the fabric under ¼˝ twice and topstitching.

AMERICAN SKY FRAMED ART

Humming the tune of *America the Beautiful* while rocking my babies gave
me lots of time to imagine the landscape that the song describes. Ever since, I
have been drawing and painting designs I call "whimsical Americana."
This simple take on Old Glory celebrates America's natural beauty.

Materials

- 8″ × 10″ silk screen
- Paper squeegee
- Acrylic screen-printing ink and acrylic base extender
- 9″ × 12″ print-making paper
- Masking tape
- Craft knife, such as an X-ACTO
- Cutting mat
- Copy paper for stencils

TIPS

- Print lots of posters at one time! Each printed piece will be one of a kind with lots of color variety.

- The paper stencil can only be used until the screen is washed, so take advantage—the posters make great gifts.

- For a marbled affect, do not thoroughly mix the extender and colors. They will mix with continued passes.

- It may take two or three prints to get the screen fully flooded and printing properly. Sometimes acrylic inks can seem a little stiff, but they warm up after a few passes.

Instructions

Refer to Screen Printing (page 59).

1 Make 2 stencils using the Stars and the Stripes patterns (page 106)—one with the stars and the other with the stripes.

2 Tape the stripe stencil to the outside of the screen. Place the screen facedown so that the top is aligned with the top of the printmaking paper.

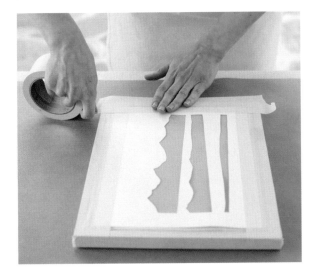

3 Mix the gradient colors directly on the screen: Spoon about 6 tablespoons of extender down the left side of the screen. Add about 1 teaspoon magenta toward the top. Add 1 teaspoon yellow and a few dabs of magenta to the bottom. Stir the colors together in the middle.

4 Print the colors. Experiment with turning the squeegee to fill the colors in the opposite direction. Use a spatula often to push the colors off the squeegee and back onto the screen. Print lots!

5 Throw away the used stencil. Wash and dry the screen.

6 Tape the star stencil onto the outside of the screen. Place the screen on top of a dry print of the stripes, lining it up with the top of the paper.

7 Mix the star color directly on the screen with 2 tablespoons base extender, ½ teaspoon cyan, and 3 dabs of magenta.

8 Print the stars.

9 Throw away the used paper and then wash the screen.

BABY BUNNY BLANKET

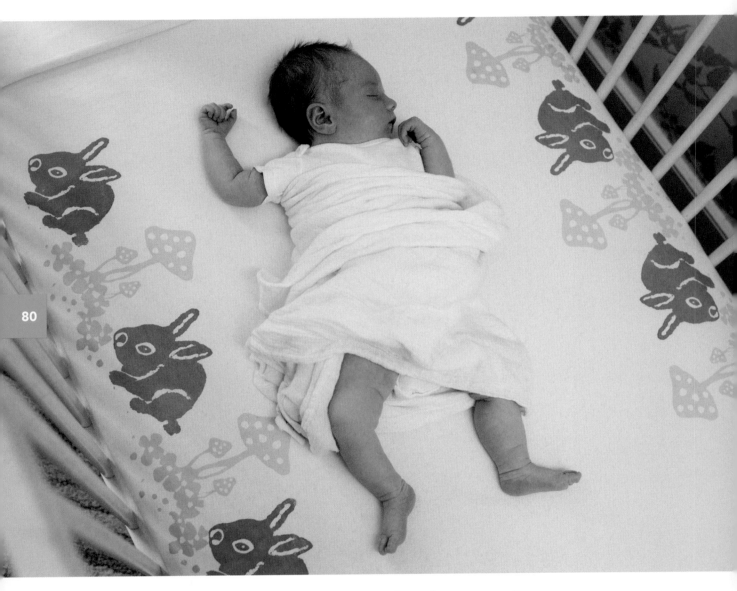

Excitement abounds when bunny nests are found in our yard!
My boys and I have built quite the wire barrier around them to
protect the babies from our dog. Their soft little bodies and
bloated tummies could not be cuter, which makes them perfect
for soft, cozy baby blankets.

Materials

- 100% cotton (preferably organic), fleece, or French jersey: 1 yard, cut to about 30″ × 40″
- 9″ × 12″ silk screen
- Screen filler
- Paintbrush
- Fabric squeegee
- Water-based textile inks and clear base extender
- Masking tape

TIP

Don't limit your design to only a blanket. Try printing on soft muslin to use as a swaddle blanket, bibs, onesies, or fitted crib sheets.

Instructions

Refer to Screen Printing (page 59).

1 Use screen filler to transfer the Bunny and the Mushroom patterns (pages 107 and 108) to opposite ends of the same screen. With the screen oriented vertically, place the bunny toward the bottom, 3″ from the left side. Fit the mushroom on the other end of the screen, facing the opposite direction.

2 Apply tape over the mushroom design, since the bunny will be printed first.

3 Mix the inks: For the bunny, mix ½ cup base extender, ½ teaspoon red, and ½ teaspoon yellow. Wait to mix the ink for the mushrooms until after you've printed all the bunnies and let them dry. For the mushrooms, you will mix ½ cup base extender, ¼ teaspoon blue, and ¼ teaspoon yellow.

4 Place the fabric flat on the worktable so that you can move around both sides.

5 Align the screen at the bottom left corner of the fabric so that the screen's edge lines up with the fabric's edge. Print the first bunny.

6 Move the screen so that the left edge is as close as possible to the bunny's tail; print again. Print both of the longer sides of the blanket—you will have 4 bunnies per side. Remove the tape and wash the screen. Allow the ink to dry.

7 Print the mushroom. Cover the bunny design on the outside of the screen with masking tape. Place the mushroom in between 2 bunnies so that the colors do not overlap. Print the design.

8 Continue moving around the fabric until you have filled in the spaces between the bunnies with mushrooms. You will have a total of 6 mushroom prints.

9 Remove the tape and wash the screen.

10 Heat set the design after the ink has dried.

11 Finish the edges by machine with an overlock stitch or by hand with a blanket stitch using embroidery floss.

BISON TOILE BANDANA

Cowgirls are just about as American as you can get, and sometimes I like to dress like one. The iconic bison perfectly adorns the corners of this bandana and looks great with my favorite cowgirl boots. This bandana is made from high-quality crafting cotton, which is readily available in uncountable colors, or try using silk for a more sophisticated look.

Materials

- High-quality crafting cotton, such as American Made Brand: 1 yard, cut to a 32″ × 32″ square
- 9″ × 12″ silk screen
- Screen filler
- Paintbrush
- Fabric squeegee
- Water-based textile inks and clear base extender
- Masking tape

Instructions

Refer to Screen Printing (page 59).

1 Transfer the Bison pattern (page 109) to the screen with screen filler.

2 Mix the ink using ⅓ cup base extender, 1 teaspoon blue, and ⅛ teaspoon red.

3 Place the fabric on the printing surface so that the corner is facing you.

4 Print the design in each corner of the bandana, about 3″ from the fabric's edge.

5 Heat set the bison after the inks are dry.

6 Leave the edges unfinished for a rustic look, or hem by turning ¼″.

TRANSFER PRINTING

Simply put, transfer printing is the process of making your own iron-on design, and it can be addictive. Powdered disperse dyes are used as paint with a watercolor effect on copy paper; after drying, they are heat transferred to polyester or nylon. These dyes do not work on natural fibers such as cotton, linen, or rayon. The dye is remarkably different in color before and after being heated, so there will be an exciting surprise on the fabric! The paper can be used multiple times until the dye appears too faded. When heated, the dye actually dissolves into the fiber, making the color exceptionally permanent.

MIXING DYE PAINTS AND CREATING TRANSFERS

Materials

- Copy paper
- Watercolor paintbrushes
- Inking plate, palette, or saucers
- Glass of water
- Disperse dyes such as PRO Transperse Dye (see Resources, page 111)

Mix the transfer dyes. Measure about ⅛ teaspoon dye powder onto a saucer or into different compartments of a paint palette. Add a few drops of water to each color.

PAINTING FLORAL DESIGNS

Paint one color at a time in flower-shaped sections with a round-tip brush. Allow the shapes to overlap and blend into clusters. After the flowers are dry, use black dye paint to add circles to each flower shape's center.

COLOR BLOCKING

Mix colors from the Mixing Dye Paints and Creating Transfers instructions (above). Using a flat-tip brush, paint colors next to each other in sections. Allow them to overlap along the edges; some blending is okay.

NOTE: Be sure to wear a dust mask when you are mixing the powders, and work in a well-ventilated room when transferring the designs to fabric.

TRANSFERRING DESIGNS

Materials

- Polyester or nylon fabric

- Dye painting on copy paper (All the paint should be dry.)

- Iron (A dry iron with no steam vents is preferable, but a steam iron set to no steam works as well.)

1 Set the iron to the appropriate heat for your fabric. Place the dry artwork facedown on the fabric.

2 Press with the iron until the desired color is reached. Move the iron over the paper, especially if the iron has steam vents. Start on a low heat setting. If the design is taking a long time to transfer, then continue to turn up the heat a half setting at a time until the desired color is reached. This could take from a few seconds to a few minutes, depending on the fabric and heat settings. Do not turn the heat too high or the fabric could melt or slump. As you iron, peel up a corner to see how the transfer is progressing.

TIPS

- Paint lots of sheets at a time. Use the sheets over and over until the dye is too faint.

- If possible, use a dry iron instead of a typical steam iron. The markings on the underside of the steam iron can transfer to your fabric if you don't move the iron around.

- Dye paintings need to be completely dry before transferring. Ironing wet paper will spread the dye across the paper, ruining the fabric.

WATERCOLOR RIBBON

These beautiful, one-of-a-kind watercolor-looking ribbons can be used to wrap a special package, tie in hair, wear as a belt, or make a bracelet. They add a personal decorative touch to a special event or party. For an array of textures and widths, try printing on different types of ribbon.

Materials

- An assortment of white or cream polyester or nylon ribbon, such as grosgrain, velvet, or satin

- PRO Transperse Dye powder or other disperse dye powder

- Watercolor paint palette

- Watercolor paintbrushes

- Copy paper

- Iron

Instructions

Refer to Transfer Printing (page 87).

1 Paint a few color block designs.

2 Heat the iron.

3 Place the ribbon flat on the worktable.

4 Place the transfer artwork facedown across the ribbon and press with the iron until the desired color is achieved.

5 Continue moving and turning the transfer paper down the ribbon until you have printed the desired length.

ABSTRACT CARPET SQUARES

Watch out old-school kindergarten rest-time carpet squares! These sophisticated tiles can do the same job in style. They can be arranged to form a completely custom rug or used individually as extra seating. They are particularly great outdoors, and your friends won't believe that you actually printed your own carpet. I used FLOR's Fedora carpet squares (see Resources, page 111) because they are budget friendly, available in the light oatmeal color, and approved for high traffic. The company is praised for its efforts toward sustainability.

Materials

- 12 or so felted carpet tiles in a light color, such as FLOR's Fedora in oatmeal

- PRO Transperse Dye powder or other disperse dye powder

- Watercolor paint palette

- Watercolor paintbrushes

- Copy paper

- Iron

Instructions

Refer to Transfer Printing (page 87).

1 Paint a few color block designs and allow them to dry.

2 Heat the iron on a low setting and check frequently while increasing the heat; the felt tends to slump easily.

3 Transfer the design, one square at a time, along one edge.

4 After you have finished printing all the tiles, arrange them on the floor as an area rug or runner.

IN THE MEADOW CURTAINS

Painting floral designs with watercolor is common practice in my studio. Making these vintage-inspired floral curtains will show you just how easy it can be! Paint a meadow to match your decor. I used a nubby polyester curtain panel in ivory because I love how the colors look over the heavy texture, but a sheer or anything 100% polyester will work.

Materials

- White or cream curtain panels—100% polyester
- PRO Transperse Dye powder or other disperse dye powder
- Watercolor paint palette
- Watercolor paintbrushes
- Scissors
- Copy paper
- Iron

Instructions

Refer to Transfer Printing (page 87).

1 Paint lots of floral designs.

2 Use scissors to cut the flower paintings into smaller pieces.

3 Transfer the designs randomly across the curtain panels.

SELLING YOUR WARES

Fortunately for home crafters, there are many outlets today for selling your wares. Please know that if you plan to do so, you must use your own designs. The patterns in this book are only for personal use, gifts, and donations to nonprofit organizations; they cannot be resold.

CRAFT SHOWS

The way I got started in selling my goods was by testing the market at craft shows. I would make a few of each design and see which sold and which struggled. The more popular designs I continued to make, while retiring the duds. Local shows that do not require travelling or a hefty booth fee are the best places to begin. As you get more experienced and learn your product, bigger shows would be the next step. Most cities have large outdoor, tented shows, such as Art Star in Philadelphia or Renegade Craft Fair in Brooklyn.

ONLINE

It seems that most makers get started, and sometimes remain with, Etsy.com. It is free to open an online store, and you immediately become part of a larger social network that can be used to promote your shop. Learning how to photograph, package, and ship are par for the course. More can be learned by exploring Etsy.com and by reading *Sewing to Sell—The Beginner's Guide to Starting a Craft Business* by Virginia Lindsay (see Resources, page 111).

100

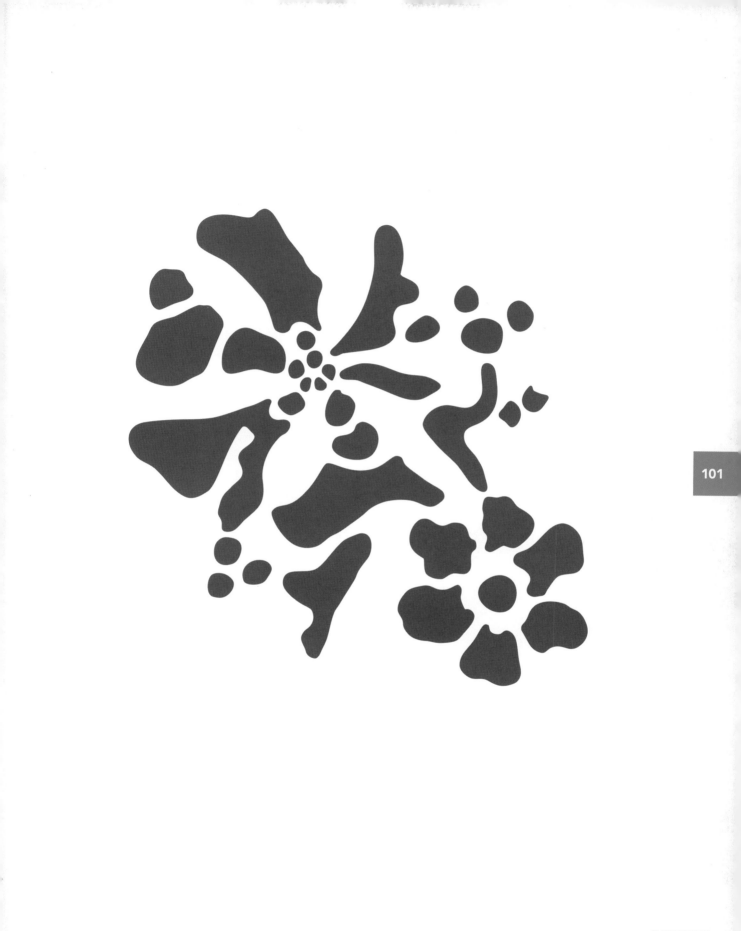

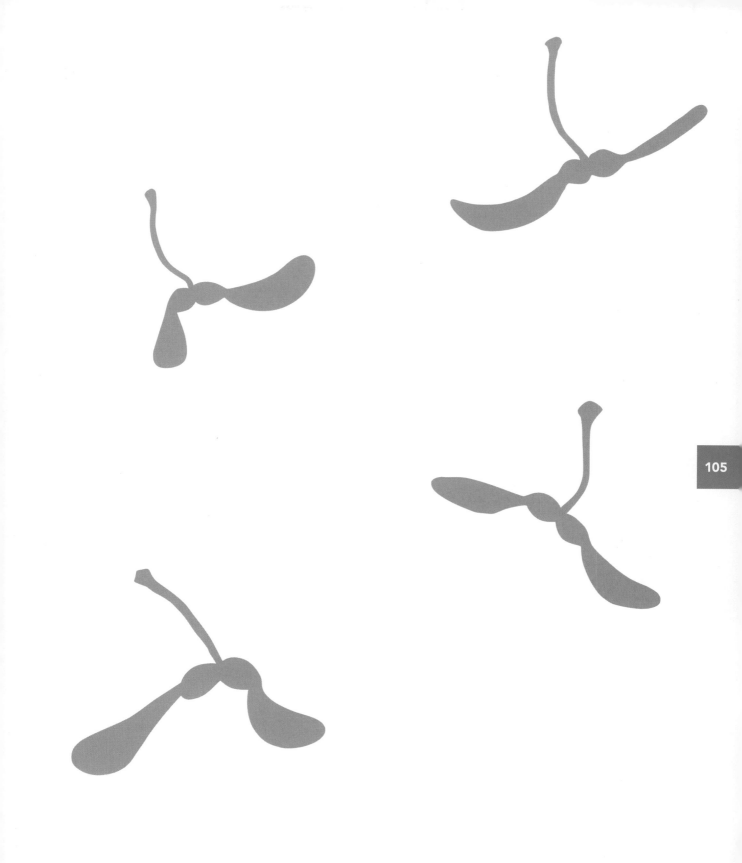

105

PATTERNSPATTERNS

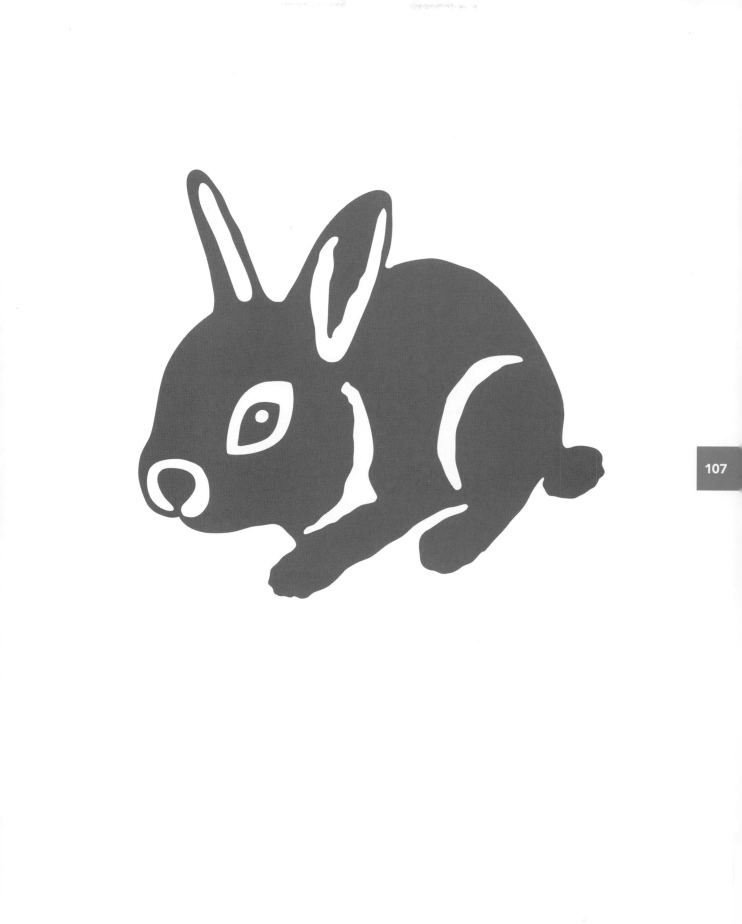

ABOUT THE AUTHOR

BETSY OLMSTED is the artist behind her textile design company, and her collections are available in top boutiques, stores, and museum shops nationwide. Crafting fabrics, luxury goods, and children's decor can be found through her licensing partners, such as Guildery, Clothworks, Oopsy Daisy, and Deny Designs, to name a few. Her expertise in printing and repeat making was founded by a Master of Science in Textiles from Philadelphia University, and she is eager to share her passion with her fans.

As a lover of life, Betsy enjoys tending her garden while snail hunting with her boys and laughing about the pesky neighborhood rodents. Cooking with local, seasonal foods is a passion, much like entertaining and creating quirky party atmospheres. As a clumsy yoga dabbler, she reminisces about her adventures in India and other curious places. Vintage furniture can sometimes become an obsession, and magazines and books abound in her house. She adores animals and fantasizes about the day when she will have a Swiss cow as a family pet. The Betsy Olmsted studio is located in historic downtown Lancaster, Pennsylvania, where Betsy turns her inspirations into colorfully whimsical designs.

RESOURCES

Carpet tiles
flor.com

Fabric and blanks for printing
Check your local fabric or craft store or buy online at:

acshomeandwork.com

clothworks.com

organiccottonplus.com

voguefabricsstore.com

Hairpin table legs
hairpinlegs.com

Printing supplies
Check your local art supply or craft store or buy online at:

dharmatrading.com

rubberstampchamp.com (tattoo inkpads)

speedballart.com

prochemicalanddye.com

Wooden cards
cardsofwood.com

Books
Sewing to Sell—The Beginner's Guide to Starting a Craft Business by Virginia Lindsay

Textile Designs: Two Hundred Years of European and American Patterns Organized by Motif, Style, Color, Layout, and Period by Susan Meller and Joost Elffers

Credits
bgcsewing.com for sewing samples

aheirloom.com for muddler (page 66)

cassandra-smith.com for painted antler (page 75)